SHORT WALKS ON THE MALVERN HILLS

by Julia Goodfellow-Smith

The Northern Hills from the west side of Herefordshire Beacon

CONTENTS

Using this guide. 4
Route summary table 6
Map key. 7
Introduction. 9
   Walking on the Malvern Hills 9
   Things to see 10
   Bases and places to stay. 11
   Travel 11

The walks

1.	Great Malvern Priory and Worcestershire Beacon	13
2.	Malvhina fountain and St Ann's Well.	19
3.	Around North Hill on Lady Howard de Walden Drive.	23
4.	Woodland and apple orchard walk	27
5.	Worcestershire Beacon from the Wyche Cutting	33
6.	British Camp Iron Age hill fort	37
7.	Black Hill.	41
8.	Wynds Point (British Camp) from Colwall	45
9.	Holy Well from Gardiner's Quarry	51
10.	The Southern Hills	57
11.	Eastnor obelisk	63
12.	St Wulstan's Nature Reserve.	67
13.	Around Malvern Common	71
14.	Malvern Community Woodland	75
15.	Old Hills.	81

Useful information. 85

USING THIS GUIDE

Routes in this book

In this book you will find a selection of easy or moderate walks suitable for almost everyone, including casual walkers and families with children, or for when you only have a short time to fill. The routes have been carefully chosen to allow you to explore the area and its attractions. Although there may be some climbs there is no challenging terrain, but do bear in mind that conditions can sometimes be wet or muddy underfoot. A route summary table is included on page 6 to help you choose the right walk.

Clothing and footwear

You won't need any special equipment to enjoy these walks. The weather in Britain can be changeable, so choose clothing suitable for the season and wear or carry a waterproof jacket. For footwear, comfortable walking boots or trainers with a good grip are best. A small rucksack for drinks, snacks and spare clothing is useful. See www.adventuresmart.uk.

Walk descriptions

At the beginning of each walk you'll find all the information you need:

- start/finish location, with postcode and a what3words address to help you find it
- parking and transport information, estimated walking time, total distance and climb
- details of public toilets available along the route and where you can get refreshments
- a summary of the key highlights of the walk and what you might see

Timings given are the time to complete the walk at a reasonable walking pace. Allow extra time for extended stops or if walking with children.

The route is described in clear, easy-to-follow directions, with each waypoint marked on an accompanying map extract. It's a good idea to read the whole of the route instructions before setting out, so that you know what to expect.

Maps, GPX files and what3words

Extracts from the OS 1:25,000 map accompany each route. GPX files for all the walks in this book are available to download at www.cicerone.co.uk/1139/gpx.

What3words is a free smartphone app which identifies every 3m square of the globe with a unique three-word address, e.g. ///destiny.cafe.sonic. For more information see https://what3words.com/products/what3words-app.

USING THIS GUIDE

Walking with children

Even young children can be surprisingly strong walkers, but every family is different and you may need to adapt the timings given in this book to take that into account. Make sure you go at the pace of the slowest member and choose a walk with an exciting objective in mind, such as a cave, waterfall or picnic spot. Many of the walks can be shortened to suit – suggestions are included at the end of the route description.

Dogs

Sheep or cattle may be found grazing on a number of these walks. Keep dogs under control at all times so that they don't scare or disturb livestock or wildlife. Cattle, particularly cows with calves, may very occasionally pose a risk to walkers with dogs. If you ever feel threatened by cattle, you should let go of your dog's lead and let it run free.

Enjoying the countryside responsibly

Enjoy the countryside and treat it with respect to protect our natural environments. Stick to footpaths and take your litter home with you. When driving, slow down on rural roads and park considerately, or better still use public transport. For more details check out www.gov.uk/countryside-code.

The Countryside Code

Respect everyone
- be considerate to those living in, working in and enjoying the countryside
- leave gates and property as you find them
- do not block access to gateways or driveways when parking
- be nice, say hello, share the space
- follow local signs and keep to marked paths unless wider access is available

Protect the environment
- take your litter home – leave no trace of your visit
- do not light fires and only have BBQs where signs say you can
- always keep dogs under control and in sight
- dog poo – bag it and bin it – any public waste bin will do
- care for nature – do not cause damage or disturbance

Enjoy the outdoors
- check your route and local conditions
- plan your adventure – know what to expect and what you can do
- enjoy your visit, have fun, make a memory

SHORT WALKS ON THE MALVERN HILLS

ROUTE SUMMARY TABLE

WALK NAME	START POINT	TIME	DISTANCE
1. Great Malvern Priory and Worcestershire Beacon	Great Malvern Priory	2hr	6.5km (4 miles)
2. Malvhina fountain and St Ann's Well	Great Malvern railway station	2hr	3.5km (2¼ miles)
3. Around North Hill on Lady Howard de Walden Drive	Belle Vue Terrace, Malvern	2hr	4km (2½ miles)
4. Woodland and apple orchard walk	West Malvern	3hr	7km (4¼ miles)
5. Worcestershire Beacon from the Wyche Cutting	Wyche Cutting	1¾hr	4km (2½ miles)
6. British Camp Iron Age hill fort	Wynds Point	1½hr	2.5km (1½ miles)
7. Black Hill	Wynds Point	1¼hr	4km (2½ miles)
8. Wynds Point (British Camp) from Colwall	Colwall railway station	2½hr	6km (3¾ miles)
9. Holy Well from Gardiner's Quarry	Gardiner's Quarry	2¼hr	6km (3¾ miles)
10. The Southern Hills	Hollybush	3hr	7.5km (4¾ miles)
11. Eastnor obelisk	Eastnor	1¾hr	5km (3 miles)
12. St Wulstan's Nature Reserve	Malvern Wells	1hr	2.5km (1½ miles)
13. Around Malvern Common	Peachfield Road, Malvern	1¾hr	3.5km (2¼ miles)
14. Malvern Community Woodland	Malvern retail park	45min	2.5km (1½ miles)
15. Old Hills	Callow End	1½hr	3.5km (2¼ miles)

MAP KEY

HIGHLIGHTS

Panoramic views and priory

Two famous fountains and Malvern's treescape

Views

Woodland, orchards and views

Summit with great views

Magnificent views and ancient hill fort

Views, bluebells in spring

Views, nature reserve and bluebells in spring

Views, woodland and a famous spring

Views, woodland and hill fort

Views, obelisk and castle

Woodland and meadows, view of the hills

Views, orchids and butterflies

Woodland

Views, woodland and horses

SYMBOLS USED ON ROUTE MAPS

(S) Start point

(F) Finish point

(SF) Start and finish at the same place

4→ Waypoint

~ Route line

~ Alternate route line

MAPPING IS SHOWN AT A SCALE OF 1:25,000

```
0 KM      0.25      0.5
|----|----|----|----|
0 miles        0.25
```

DOWNLOAD THE GPX FILES FOR FREE AT
www.cicerone.co.uk/1139/GPX

The northern hills

INTRODUCTION

The Malvern Hills rising from the Severn Plain

The Malvern Hills rise spectacularly from the low rolling landscape of the Severn Plain to the east and the wooded hills of Herefordshire to the west. The Malverns are not high, but because they stand out in the landscape, they can be wild and invigorating. Trees flank the lower slopes, thinning to grassland at the top of most of the hills, which creates the opportunity for far-reaching views. Bluebells swathe the west side, apple orchards bloom to the north and flower-rich meadows adorn the valley to the east.

Walking on the Malvern Hills

From steep paths straight up to the top of hills to gentle strolls through the meadows below, the Malvern Hills have everything you need for fabulous walking. For this book, we have chosen 15 popular walks that are easy to follow, offer incredible views and give you the opportunity to experience the best of the area.

The Malvern Hills also have some of the most pleasant weather in the country – drier and sunnier than average. However, even if it appears calm at the bottom of the hills, it can be seriously breezy when you near the ridge. The temperature at the top of the hills is around 2–3 degrees lower than at the foot, so it is always a good idea to carry a jacket.

The paths on the hills are mainly dry and are well kept, although many have a loose stony surface. There are some exceptions, and these are clearly identified in the walk descriptions.

Redundant quarries abound on the hills, from tiny workings to large commercial sites. Many now form interesting wildlife habitats. Beware the quarry lakes; these are spring-fed and can be deep, cold and dangerous to swim in.

The Malvern Hills have many water fountains and springs, known locally as 'wells', and the walks in this book visit some of them. Although many locals drink from the wells, there is a risk that the water is contaminated, so it is not recommended. The water from the Malvhina fountain on Bellevue Island, however, is filtered and therefore usually safe to drink.

Each of the habitats on the hills supports different birds. You might hear the call of a cuckoo in May and June, see yellow flashes from a flock of goldfinches or the looping flight of a green woodpecker. Skylarks nest on the commons and some of the upland grassland areas – listen out for their distinctive song, heard high in the sky as they try to distract attention from their nests in the grass. Birds of prey like buzzards and kestrels are commonly seen and occasionally red kites soar overhead. Goshawks and peregrine falcons also live on the hills, the latter sometimes nesting on the quarry faces.

Things to see

The main attraction for people visiting the Malvern Hills is the incredible vista over the surrounding area. On a clear day, you can see the Bristol Channel to the south, the Black Mountains in Wales to the west, Long Mynd in Shropshire to the north and the Cotswolds to the east. The topograph on Worcestershire Beacon shows you where to look for each.

The Malvern Hills GeoCentre is a great place to visit if you want to understand more about the geology of the hills.

One of the many benches on the hills (Walk 7)

North Hill (furthest right) seen from Worcestershire Beacon (Walk 3)

Until Victorian times, Malvern was a small town housing a community of Benedictine monks. During the 19th century, it became a spa town and had a population and housing boom. Great Malvern Priory has misericords (part of the choir stalls) that date from the 14th and 15th centuries, an impressive range of stained-glass windows and a stunning collection of medieval tiles. A few miles south, Little Malvern Priory contains one of only two 15th-century stained-glass windows in the country that depict Edward IV and the young prince who became Edward V.

The market town of Ledbury contains many independent shops and a 17th-century market hall. Nearby is Eastnor Castle and Gardens.

Bases and places to stay

The biggest base in the area is Great Malvern, usually just called 'Malvern', where there is a wide range of accommodation. The town boasts a priory, spa, museum, three theatres and a cinema, as well as pubs, cafes and restaurants.

The smaller market town of Ledbury has accommodation, a theatre, museum and a range of independent shops, cafes and pubs. There is also a hotel in the village of Colwall, which has a limited range of local facilities.

Travel

Many people travel to Malvern by car, as it is only a 20-minute drive from the M5 and M50 and bus services beyond the bigger towns are infrequent. Frequent train services run to Malvern Link and Great Malvern. Colwall and Ledbury also have train stations. Several of the walks start at or near public transport links, as detailed in the walk information.

Great Malvern Priory seen from the hills

WALK 1
Great Malvern Priory and Worcestershire Beacon

Start/finish	Great Malvern Priory
Locate	WR14 2AY ///views.field.spark
Cafes/pubs	Pubs and cafes in Malvern, cafe at St Ann's Well
Transport	Train to Great Malvern station, 800m from priory. Bus from Hereford and Worcester
Parking	Small car park off St Ann's Road, larger car park on Priory Road, limited on-street parking in town centre
Toilets	Next to theatre on Grange Road, above Waitrose on Edith Walk and at St Ann's Well

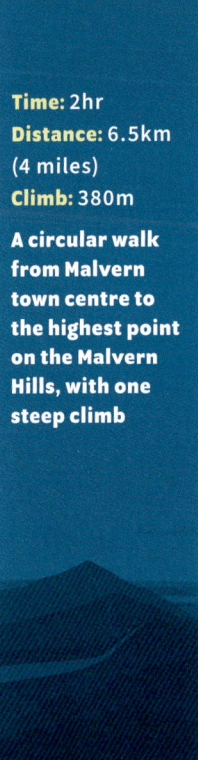

Time: 2hr
Distance: 6.5km (4 miles)
Climb: 380m

A circular walk from Malvern town centre to the highest point on the Malvern Hills, with one steep climb

A steep climb onto the hills is worth the effort as the views open up, first across the Severn Plain to the Cotswolds, then to the Black Mountains in Wales, and finally a full 360 degrees. After visiting the summit of Worcestershire Beacon, the route drops down into cool woodland, past one of Malvern's famous springs before returning to Great Malvern Priory.

View south from the west side of Worcestershire Beacon

SHORT WALKS ON THE MALVERN HILLS

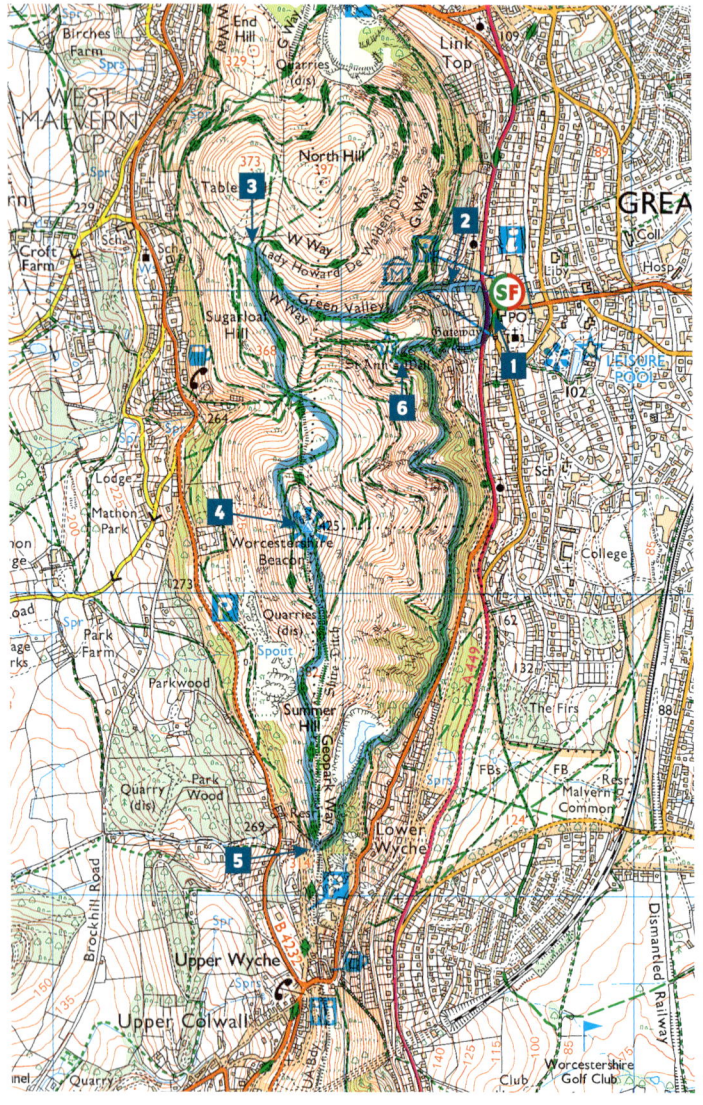

The track meandering towards the summit of Worcestershire Beacon

1 From the end of the drive leading to the priory, head up Church Street. Climb the steps to the left of the statue of Sir Edward Elgar and turn left at the top to the Malvhina fountain. Designed by Rose Garrard in the 1990s, the fountain is fed from three different sources on the hills. The water is UV filtered, so is usually safe to drink. Use the pelican crossing above the fountain and turn right past the shops. Turn left immediately after The Unicorn pub up a steep hill.

Authors C S Lewis and J R R Tolkien frequented The Unicorn when visiting Malvern. Were Malvern's gas lamps the inspiration for the entrance to Narnia? Did the hills provide inspiration for the White Mountains? Some certainly like to think so.

2 Where the road bends to the left, continue straight up Happy Valley. A little way up, a small stream flows to the left of the track. Follow this stream to its source and then continue uphill until you reach a track running around the hill.

3 Turn left and head approximately south until you reach a round stone waymarker at a junction of many paths. The summit of Worcestershire Beacon is straight ahead, but our route takes the wide track diagonally left at about 10 o'clock. Follow this track as it meanders towards and around the summit, gently rising until it crests the hill and arrives at the top of **Worcestershire Beacon**. The trig point and toposcope are a few metres to the left.

SHORT WALKS ON THE MALVERN HILLS

Great Malvern Priory seen from Rosebank Gardens

At 425m Worcestershire Beacon is the highest point of the Malvern Hills. The topograph details the peaks visible on a clear day, including Long Mynd, the Cotswold escarpment and the Black Mountains.

4 Head east off the summit (Malvern is visible at the bottom of the hill) and turn right onto the track that heads downhill towards the south. The Iron Age hill fort at British Camp can be seen ahead in the middle distance. Continue past **Summer Hill** to the next round waymarker labelled 'Goldmine'.

ⓘ *Many eminent Victorians visited Malvern, including Florence Nightingale, Charles Dickens and Alfred Lord Tennyson.*

5 Take a sharp left downhill into the woods. As the path rises, fork right between the low mossy wall and the bank. When the path reaches a grassy clearing, take a small detour into Earnslaw Quarry by following the path a little further and to the left. The lake in this quarry is home to water lilies and, occasionally, kingfishers. Retrace your steps to the grassy area

WALK 1 – GREAT MALVERN PRIORY AND WORCESTERSHIRE BEACON

On the top of Worcestershire Beacon

and take the path leading steeply downhill. After about 400m, as you near a road, continue left on the path to reach **St Ann's Well**, just over 1km further on, where there is another spring, a cafe and toilets.

6 Follow the zigzag drive downhill from the cafe. At the junction with St Ann's Road, turn right then bear left almost immediately and descend the steps into Rosebank Gardens and back to the priory, which is clearly visible from here.

> **– To shorten**
>
> For a walk that will take around 45min, at the stone waymarker between Waypoints 3 and 4, turn left and take the second path to the left down to St Ann's Well.

Malvhina spring on Bellevue Island

WALK 2
Malvhina fountain and St Ann's Well

Start/finish	Great Malvern railway station
Locate	WR14 3AL ///vocal.type.spice
Cafes/pubs	Cafe at start and at St Ann's Well, pubs and cafes in Malvern
Transport	Train to Great Malvern station
Parking	At station and on-street nearby
Toilets	At station, next to theatre on Grange Road and at St Ann's Well

Time: 2hr
Distance 3.5km (2¼ miles)
Climb: 175m

Visit two of Malvern's famous fountains and admire its amazing trees on this steep walk through town

A perfect introduction to Malvern's architecture, grand priory church and unique treescape, and to two of its iconic fountains, Malvhina and St Ann's Well. Although this figure-of-eight route is undoubtedly steep, most of the walk is on tarmac and there are opportunities to sit and take a break at various points. Take a short detour into Rosebank Gardens for the best view of the remarkable buzzards and skylark sculptures.

Victorian residence on Avenue Road with its 'status symbol' cedar tree

SHORT WALKS ON THE MALVERN HILLS

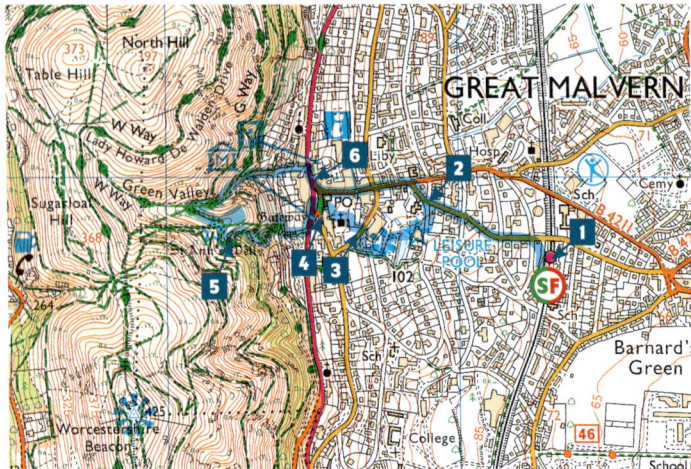

Start by taking a peek at the railway station itself. It was designed by prominent local architect Edmund Wallace Elmslie and retains many of its Victorian features, including highly decorated columns supporting the canopy.

1 With your back to the ticket office, turn right for a few paces, cross the car park and ascend the steps into Imperial Gardens. Turn right onto the path and follow it round to the far-left corner of the gardens. Cross Imperial Road to follow Avenue Road uphill as far as a huge monkey puzzle tree at the third crossroads. Look up to appreciate the splendour of the trees as you walk.

2 At the crossroads turn left into Priory Road. Opposite the car park, turn right and right again past the entrance to the **leisure centre**, up a few steps and left into Priory Park. Follow the path to the left then cross the bridge over the lake. Head uphill between the bandstand and a magnificent Corsican pine. Follow the paths around the left side of the theatre to reach the road.

3 Cross Grange Road and pass a barrier to follow a path to **Great Malvern Priory**. Skirt round the church. Take the short flight of steps opposite the main entrance towards a medieval cross, turn left through an archway and up another short flight of steps to the road.

WALK 2 – MALVHINA FOUNTAIN AND ST ANN'S WELL

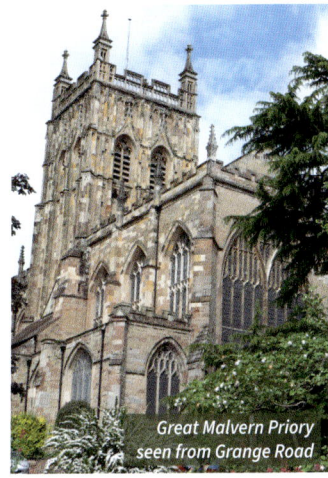

Great Malvern Priory seen from Grange Road

Great Malvern Priory was established in 1085 as an order of Benedictine monks and extended in the 15th century. After centuries of neglect, the church was restored by the Victorians. This history is reflected in the features inside, including medieval tiles, stained glass from different eras and a Victorian ceiling.

4 Head diagonally right across the road onto Bellevue Island and up to the Malvhina fountain. Cross Bellevue Terrace above the fountain and turn left. Views over the Severn Plain are now opening up to your left. Turn right into Rosebank Gardens and up the 99 steps ahead. At the top of the steps, continue uphill to a junction of small roads. Take the second left, signposted 'To the hills'. This is a steep, winding drive that leads to **St Ann's Well** and cafe.

ⓘ *The Victorians flocked to Malvern for the water. It was used to treat skin complaints and poured over the body to stimulate blood circulation.*

St Ann's Well

SHORT WALKS ON THE MALVERN HILLS

5 Take the stone track behind the cafe and climb up to a grassy knoll with fabulous views across the Severn Plain. From here, return to the track and turn right downhill into a wooded valley. Follow the track steeply to the right where it becomes a tarmac drive and continue downhill until you reach the pedestrian crossing on the main road. Cross, turn right, then fork left into Church Lane.

6 Follow this road downhill across the traffic lights. After about 350m, turn right opposite a large house called The Portland. Follow Avenue Road downhill back to the station.

> **– To shorten**
> Start and finish your walk at the car park on Priory Road close to Waypoint 2 to shorten the walk by about 20min.

Malvern's amazing trees

During Malvern's heyday as a spa town, Victorian plant-hunters were exploring the world and bringing exotic tree seeds back with them. Planting a giant redwood or monkey puzzle in your garden was a true sign of wealth that Malvern property owners embraced enthusiastically. It's hard to imagine now, but when many of these trees were planted as saplings only a couple of metres tall, Malvern had little tree cover. It would have been a busy, noisy and dusty town from all the quarrying and construction work. Did those same Victorians realise what a wonderful legacy they were leaving?

One of Malvern's amazing trees – a giant redwood on Avenue Road

WALK 3
Around North Hill on Lady Howard de Walden Drive

Start/finish	*The Unicorn pub, Belle Vue Terrace, Malvern*
Locate	*WR14 4PZ ///verge.switch.throw*
Cafes/pubs	*Pubs and cafes in Malvern*
Transport	*Train to Great Malvern station, about 1km from start*
Parking	*Small public car park behind The Unicorn, larger car park on Priory Road, limited on-street parking in town centre*
Toilets	*Next to theatre on Grange Road and above Waitrose on Edith Walk*

Time: 2hr
Distance: 4km (2½ miles)
Climb: 275m

A steep but rewarding climb from Malvern onto the north end of the hills, with far-reaching views

The ascent from the town centre onto the Malvern Hills is steep, but once on the hills, the route follows an undulating carriage track around Table Hill and North Hill, created for Lady Howard de Walden to take the air without expending too much energy. Views extend over End Hill, the most northerly hill in the range, as far as Long Mynd in Shropshire.

Lady Howard de Walden Drive encircling North Hill

SHORT WALKS ON THE MALVERN HILLS

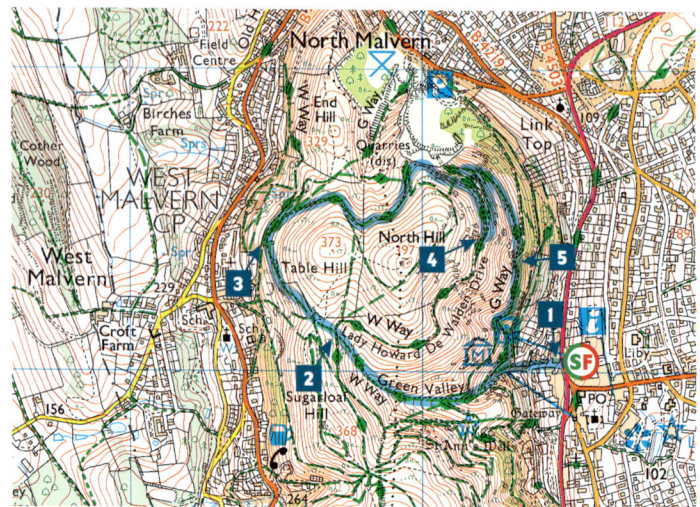

1 From The Unicorn pub, head steeply up St Ann's Road. When the road bends to the left, continue straight uphill past the cul-de-sac sign. Keep the stream on your left until its source and then continue uphill. By this point, the tarmac drive has turned into a rough stone track. Where the track opens out into a grassy ride, bear left on a narrower path through the trees to another track. This is Lady Howard de Walden Drive.

> In Victorian times, visitors to Malvern would take donkey rides up this route onto the hills. That option is no longer available and we have to rely on our own leg-power to reach the top.

2 Continue diagonally across the track to the top of the rise ahead, where someone has thoughtfully placed a couple of benches for anyone who needs a rest or wants to admire the view. The hills of Herefordshire roll away ahead towards the Black Mountains of Wales, and the Severn Plain stretches out behind. Continue straight ahead along the stony path, shortly passing another bench on your right. The village of West Malvern with the grand Regents' Theological College is visible down to the left. Arrive at a junction of paths.

3 Continue round the hill to the right, rising gently. You are now on Lady Howard de Walden Drive. The bench

WALK 3 – AROUND NORTH HILL ON LADY HOWARD DE WALDEN DRIVE

Small quarry on the west side of North Hill

at the top affords great views to the north over End Hill and as far as Long Mynd in Shropshire on a clear day. As the path continues around **North Hill**, the Severn Plain comes back into view with the whaleback of Bredon Hill rising on the far side and the Cotswold escarpment further south.

From this vantage point, you can see the variety of trees that were planted across Malvern by the Victorians. In those days, having a tree in your garden that had recently been discovered by plant hunters was a real status symbol. Many have now matured to create this unusual treescape.

4 Leave Lady Howard de Walden Drive at a waymarker post on the right with three arrows pointing downhill. Turn left down a couple of steps onto this narrower path that zigzags down the hill to reach a junction with a wider track.

5 Continue straight ahead past a rocky outcrop on your right, with the hill sloping down to your left. Take the left fork downhill through the trees. At the next fork, take the middle option directly ahead. When you reach the tarmac drive, turn left to retrace your steps back down to the town centre.

Enjoying the view of End Hill

View of End Hill from the north

WALK 4
Woodland and apple orchard walk

Start/finish	Westminster Bank, West Malvern
Locate	WR14 4AY ///forgot.booth.abstracts
Cafes/pubs	Sugarloaf Cafe at start, pub in West Malvern
Transport	Infrequent bus 675 from Malvern (St James's and The Abbey stop)
Parking	On road – Westminster Bank or nearby
Toilets	No public toilets on route

Time: 3hr
Distance: 7km (4¼ miles)
Climb: 285m

A delightful walk through an old, coppiced woodland to an apple orchard, with some steep climbs

Worcestershire is famed for its apples – and its cider. This walk takes you through what is now a peaceful woodland but was once a hive of industrial activity, with small-scale quarries and lime kilns, to one of the area's many apple orchards. If you time it right (usually in May), you will be walking through apple blossom confetti. This walk includes some steep climbs.

A glorious carpet of wood anemones in spring

SHORT WALKS ON THE MALVERN HILLS

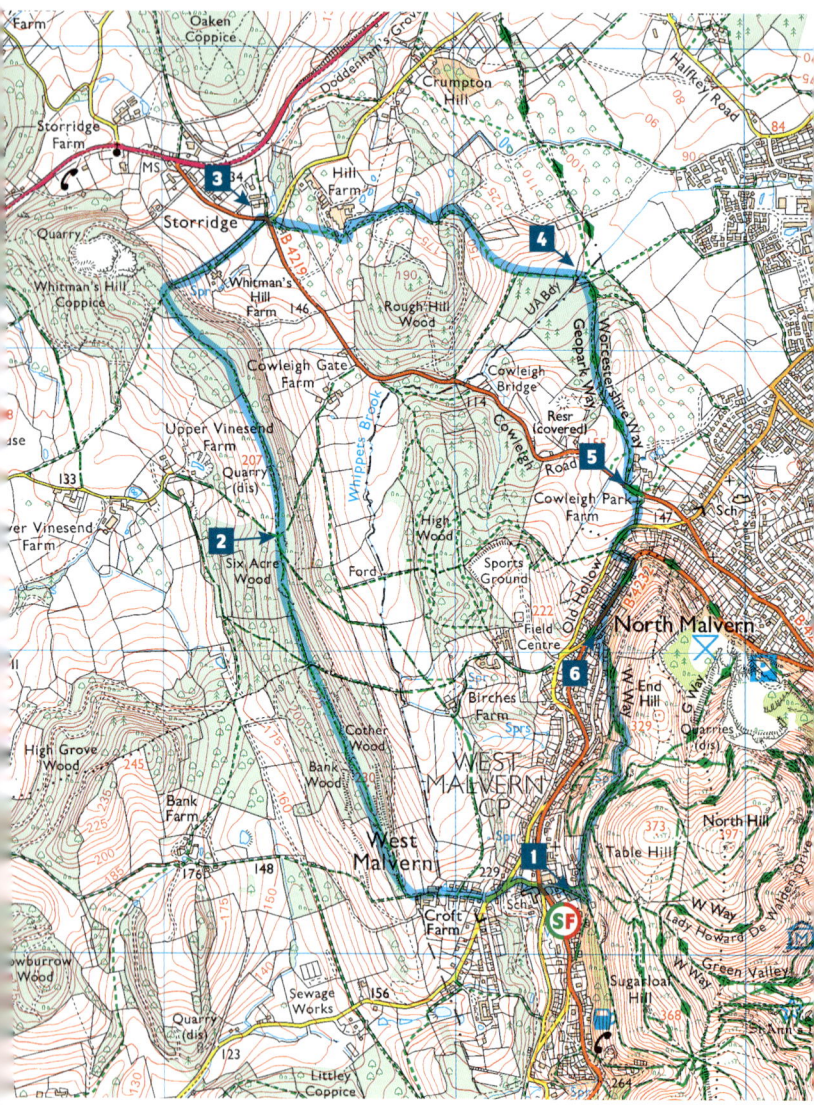

WALK 4 – WOODLAND AND APPLE ORCHARD WALK

1 From Westminster Bank, head straight downhill, crossing West Malvern Road onto Croft Bank. On the left-hand bend just past Teapot House, turn right onto Croft Farm Drive. Beyond the buildings of **Croft Farm** and with a field directly ahead, follow the track to the right and through a gate into woodland. Stay on this track through **Six Acre Wood**, ignoring smaller paths to left and right, until you reach a field on the left.

> Lime kilns once operated in these woods. You will see evidence of the limestone quarries to the side of the path, and many of the trees were coppiced (cut to ground level to promote regrowth) to provide fuel for the kilns.

2 The path passes this field and another before diving back into woodland. At the next field, follow the path that skirts it to the right. At the end of this field, continue straight ahead. About 90m further, there is a junction of paths. Turn right downhill to cross a stile. Continue down the slope, over another stile and along the drive away from **Whitman's Hill Farm** to a road.

3 Cross the road. Take the pedestrian gate next to the wide farm shop gate and follow the gravel track behind the building. Where the track bends right, continue straight ahead through a wide gap in the hedge into the orchard and uphill to the corner of the evergreen hedge. Turn right

Coppiced trees in Six Acre Wood

Harvest time in the orchard

onto the track and then left onto the main farm drive. With **Hill Farm** on your left, take the right fork. There are a couple of rows of apple trees between you and the farmhouse. Follow the track as it bears right past a house on the left and then downhill into woodland. Just before the track ends at another orchard, turn right along the edge of the wood. Cross the stile into a field. Look up for a stunning view of End Hill. Head down the shallow valley, curving left between the field and an orchard towards the bottom of the slope to reach a stream.

4 Cross the stream, turn left and then first right through a gate. Join the **Worcestershire Way** and Geopark Way to follow the path uphill between the orchard and woodland. At the top of the orchard, continue on the track through some trees then towards the Malvern Hills to the road, keeping the agricultural shed and timber-framed house on your left.

5 At the road, turn left. After a few metres, cross to Earl Beauchamp's Fountain. Just past the fountain, take the stepped footpath up to another road (Old Hollow). Turn right along the road, then a few metres after the wood-clad house, take the steps on the left up to West Malvern Road. Turn right and follow the road for about 300m. Just before this road converges with **Old Hollow** on the right, turn left onto the footpath and then steeply uphill onto Lamb Bank. Where the road bends to the right, continue steeply uphill to a gate.

WALK 4 – WOODLAND AND APPLE ORCHARD WALK

6 Through the gate, turn right onto the path. Keeping **End Hill** to your left, continue on this path for some distance until it joins a track and comes close to buildings on the right. At a junction of tracks just beyond the buildings, turn sharp right down to the starting point.

> **– To shorten**
>
> To avoid the final climb back onto the hills and save around 15min, stay on West Malvern Road, which will bring you back to your starting point.

Orchard country

Some 29 apple varieties originated from Worcestershire, which, with Herefordshire and Gloucestershire, formed the core of England's tree fruit farming in the 19th century. Much of the fruit grown in the area now is destined to be pulped and fermented into cider. Pears, plums and cherries were also grown here. The symbol of Worcestershire is the black pear, as sported by the Worcester Bowmen at the Battle of Agincourt and the Worcestershire cricket team today.

Apples ripening in an orchard

The topograph on Worcestershire Beacon

WALK 5

Worcestershire Beacon from the Wyche Cutting

Start/finish	*Wyche Cutting*
Locate	*WR14 4EH ///laying.engraving.glitter*
Cafes/pubs	*Cafe at Malvern Hills GeoCentre, pub at Wyche Cutting*
Transport	*Infrequent bus 675 from Malvern (Old Wyche Road stop)*
Parking	*Upper Beacon Road car park*
Toilets	*At Wyche Cutting behind bus stop*

This walk takes the easiest route up Worcestershire Beacon, the highest point of the Malvern Hills. The views from the top are stunning and the topograph will help you to identify what you are looking at. The paths up are all wide and fairly even underfoot. The return leg is via smaller but still well-maintained paths on the west side of the hills.

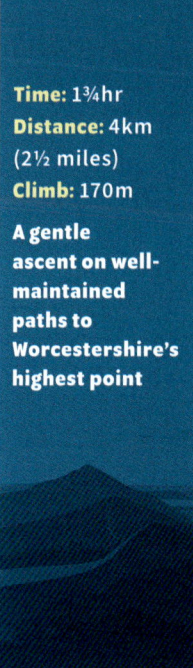

Time: 1¾hr
Distance: 4km (2½ miles)
Climb: 170m

A gentle ascent on well-maintained paths to Worcestershire's highest point

The path leading up to Worcestershire Beacon

SHORT WALKS ON THE MALVERN HILLS

1 Take the tarmac drive uphill beyond the end of the car park. Stay on the track for close to 1km as it passes the 'Goldmine' circular stone waymarker and skirts around **Summer Hill** on the right, always climbing gently upwards. Come to a dip between Summer Hill and Worcestershire Beacon, where the path splits three ways.

2 All three paths reach the summit, but our route takes the left fork, a track that gently sweeps up the west side of the hill. At a junction of paths, turn right, then left to the trig point and toposcope on **Worcestershire Beacon**.

3 From the summit continue to head north. Malvern can be seen down to your right and North Hill ahead in the distance. After a short steep and rocky descent, the path drops more gently. You are aiming for the unruly octopus of paths converging in a dip between the hills, where there's another round stone waymarker.

4 At this waymarker, you can follow signs towards Sugarloaf Hill to lengthen the walk. To continue on the main route, turn left signposted 'The Dingle'. Keep left onto the path around the hill, with the steep valley on your right. After about 350m, where paths

The stone waymarker at the 'octopus of paths'

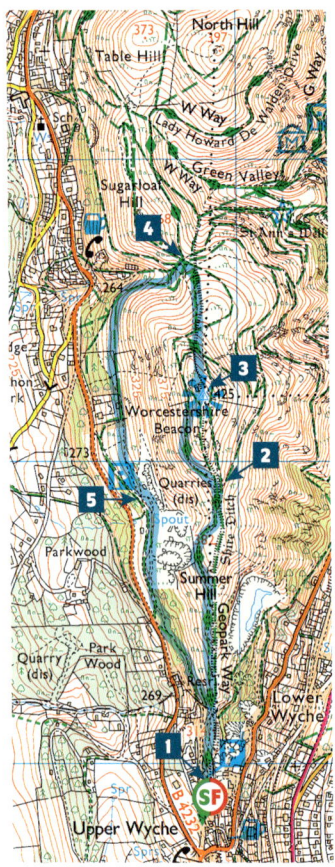

WALK 5 – WORCESTERSHIRE BEACON FROM THE WYCHE CUTTING

cross under some old sycamores, turn left onto a path that gently rises for a short distance before flattening out. This path crosses an open area, then skirts around a garden before meeting a gravel drive. Continue on the drive in the same direction until you reach a small car park.

View south from the summit

5 Cross the car park and take the stony path along the side of the hill. Ignore the steps up to the left after a few metres. Just after a disused quarry entrance set back to the left, take the right option at the three-way fork. Pass a green metal gate, then turn left onto the tarmac lane. After about 30m, by another parking area and before the lane reaches the road, take the first path on the left. Keep left at the fork to continue gently uphill. At the T-junction of paths, turn right. At the next fork, turn left and continue uphill to the round stone waymarker at Goldmine. Turn right to return to the car park.

− To shorten

Turn around at the trig point and retrace your steps back to the start. This will reduce the length of the walk by around 1km (20min).

+ To lengthen

At Waypoint 4, walk around or over Sugarloaf Hill (waymarked), returning to the same point to continue on the route. This will add about 1km (25min) to the walk.

Worcestershire Beacon

From Norman times, beacons were lit on hilltops to warn of invasion and call upon local people to take up arms, as it was the fastest way to communicate. Worcestershire Beacon has been used for just this purpose, most notably to warn of the arrival of the Spanish Armada in 1588. These days, beacons are lit on the hill to celebrate key events, such as Queen Elizabeth II's Platinum Jubilee in June 2022.

The northernmost part of the hill fort

WALK 6
British Camp Iron Age hill fort

Start/finish	British Camp car park near Wynds Point
Locate	WR13 6DW ///ratio.polished.rents
Cafes/pubs	Hotel and refreshment kiosk at start
Transport	None nearby
Parking	British Camp car park. If full, use Black Hill car park on other side of hotel
Toilets	Near Malvern Hills Hotel behind the kiosk

Time: 1½hr
Distance: 2.5km (1½ miles)
Climb: 125m

A walk up and around Herefordshire Beacon and the British Camp hill fort, with panoramic views over three counties

British Camp is an Iron Age hill fort and the highest point in Herefordshire. This short walk gives magnificent views across Herefordshire, Worcestershire and Gloucestershire, and along the length of the Malvern Hills. It uses well-made paths, and there are some steep ascents and descents. This is a popular site for picnics, although it is usually breezy at the top – a windproof jacket is recommended.

The Malvern Hills Hotel opposite British Camp car park

Enjoying the view over the northern hills

1 Leave the car park by the gate at the top of the slope near the information board. The path rises steeply with the car park below and to the left. At the first junction of paths, turn sharp right, following the stone sign to British Camp. Continue uphill on this path and turn sharp right again just before the crest of the rise onto a gravel and grass track around the ramparts to a crossing of paths.

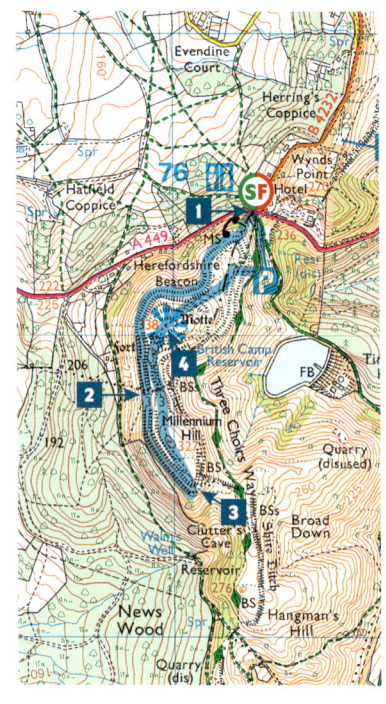

> Behind you is a view north along the Malvern Hills. The nearest is Black Hill, followed by Pinnacle Hill with the long ridge. Beyond the dip, the biggest hill is Worcestershire Beacon with Sugar Loaf Hill visible beyond that.

2 Continue along the rampart – one of the concentric rings of

WALK 6 – BRITISH CAMP IRON AGE HILL FORT

ditches and ridges that protected the hill fort. Herefordshire is rolling off to your right, and the obelisk at Eastnor (see Walk 11) is visible ahead. Carry on until the path bends to the left and meets a gravel path with steps.

3 Turn left up the steps and climb to the first summit, **Millennium Hill**. Follow the clear ridge path up to **Herefordshire Beacon**, the highest point of the hill fort (and Herefordshire).

4 From the top of the hill, follow the rough man-made path with steps downhill. Turn right down a flight of concrete steps and continue downhill. Veer left at the junction, pass a bench and then fork right to return to the car park.

British Camp

Imagine being one of the people cutting these ditches by hand! The ramparts were created by digging into the slope and piling up the debris on the outside edge, forming a steep ridge. This was initially done in two phases of construction in the Iron Age. Over a thousand years later, in medieval times, significant additional work was done on the ditches, forming the ringwork we see today. It is likely that the building that used to stand within the ringworks was a hunting lodge.

The distinctive ringwork of ditches and ridges on British Camp

Path through the trees

WALK 7
Black Hill

Start/finish	Black Hill car park near Wynds Point
Locate	WR13 6DW ///chickens.ferrying.cloth
Cafes/pubs	Hotel and refreshment kiosk near start, cafe about 100m west of Waypoint 4
Transport	None nearby
Parking	Black Hill car park. If full, use British Camp car park on other side of hotel
Toilets	Near Malvern Hills Hotel behind kiosk

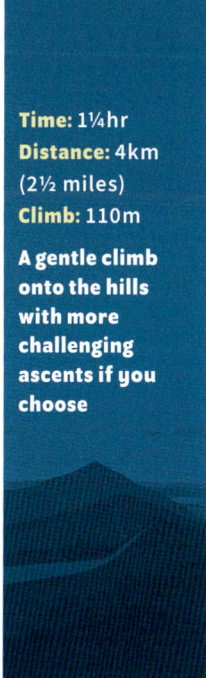

Time: 1¼hr
Distance: 4km (2½ miles)
Climb: 110m

A gentle climb onto the hills with more challenging ascents if you choose

You can make this walk as easy or hard as you like. It starts on a wheelchair-accessible path with a gentle gradient to a dip in the hills with far-reaching views east and west. The next stage takes you up Black Hill, one of the smaller climbs on the Malverns. Following that is Pinnacle Hill, a far greater challenge. Both have easier options to one side.

View from the top of the wheelchair-accessible path

Walking along the side of Pinnacle Hill

1 Turn left onto the wheelchair-accessible path at the top of the car park and climb gently to a grassy dip between two hills. Look down to the left for a glorious display of bluebells in spring. Continuing in the same direction, fork right to the top of **Black Hill** or left to walk around the side.

2 At the next dip between hills, follow the path around the left (west) side of **Pinnacle Hill**. If you are feeling very energetic you can fork right to walk to the top, but bear in mind that what you can see from here is a 'false summit' – there is more! After about 1km, the two paths re-join before the next hill (**Jubilee Hill**). There is a stand of trees immediately to the left of the path, known locally as 'Little Switzerland'.

3 Turn left downhill just before the stand of trees and follow this path to the road. For the Kettle Sings cafe, take the small road downhill from the car park entrance, signposted 'The Chase Inn'. After 70m, fork left onto the cafe's drive.

4 Turn left through the car park (right if you are returning from the cafe) and take the flat path at the far end. At a fork by a bench, take the smaller path on the right, which is more or less flat. At the bench dedicated to Dorothy Kate Shorland, take the left fork uphill to continue in the same direction, into the trees. Join the bigger path heading in the same direction to return to the car park.

Trees at 'Little Switzerland'

WALK 7 – BLACK HILL

━ To shorten
For a walk that takes 30min, at Waypoint 2, after descending from Black Hill, turn left to follow the path back to the car park.

✛ To lengthen
Walk along the path skirting the road and Malvern Hills Hotel for around 450m to reach British Camp car park and add on Walk 6 to the top of British Camp. The total length of the combined walk is 7.5km (3hr).

ⓘ *When there's a gentle easterly breeze, fog can build up against the hills. Sometimes, the tops are in sun and offer glorious views over the moisture-draped landscape.*

Common lizards on the Malvern Hills

An area of trees just to the south of Little Switzerland has been felled to create a habitat for common lizards. On a warm day between spring and autumn, you might find one basking in the sun on the path, warming itself up so it can hunt. Although they are reptiles, common lizards incubate their eggs inside their bodies and give birth to live young. Over the winter months, they hibernate under rocks or fallen logs, re-emerging when the weather warms up.

Enjoying a rest

WALK 8
Wynds Point (British Camp) from Colwall

Time: 2½hr
Distance: 6km (3¾ miles)
Climb: 195m

A circular walk from Colwall station to the hotel at British Camp, returning along the west side of the hills

Start/finish	*Colwall railway station*
Locate	*WR13 6RN ///barefoot.affair.mirroring*
Cafes/pubs	*Pub, cafes and hotel in Colwall, hotel and refreshment kiosk at Wynds Point*
Transport	*Train to Colwall station, bus from Malvern and Ledbury (Station Turn stop)*
Parking	*At railway station or nearby on street*
Toilets	*At Wynds Point near Malvern Hills Hotel*

A slightly more adventurous outing with some steep uphill sections. Passing through woods, meadows and fields, this walk packs a lot into a short distance, including a nature reserve, great views of British Camp Iron Age hill fort and across Herefordshire, and a spectacular display of bluebells in spring. The route can be muddy in places.

Walking along the side of Black Hill

SHORT WALKS ON THE MALVERN HILLS

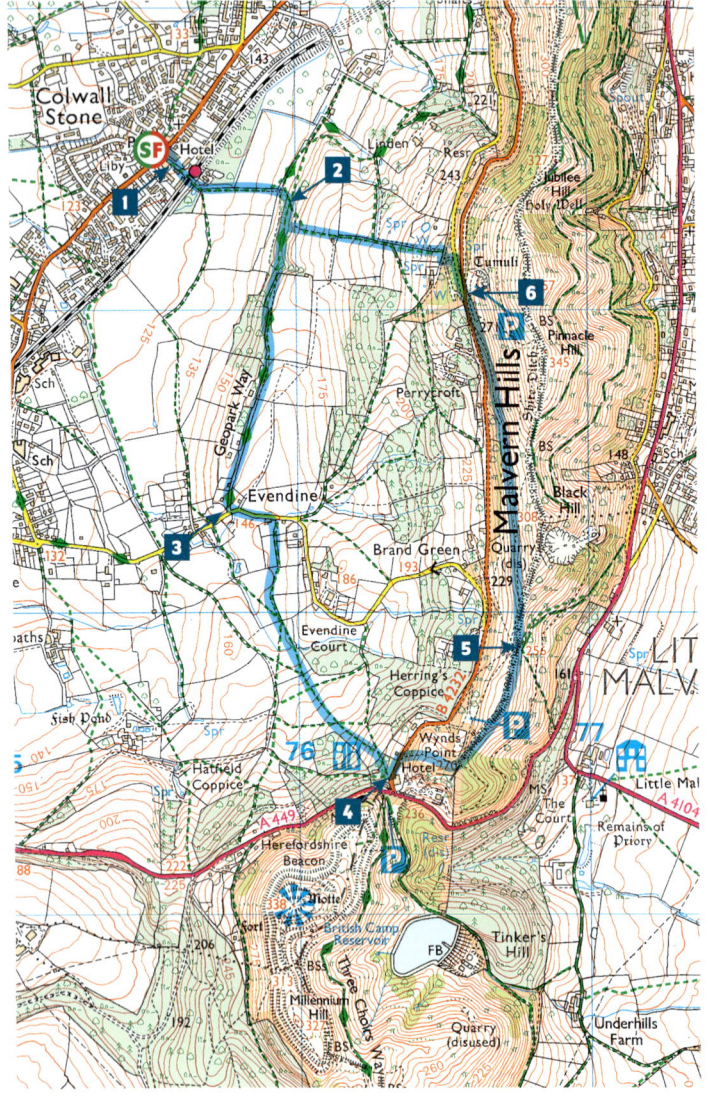

WALK 8 – WYNDS POINT (BRITISH CAMP) FROM COLWALL

The track leading to the tarmac drive approaching Evendine

1 From the car park, cross the railway bridge. Pass the Charlie Ballard Nature Reserve on your right and a sign for Station Cottages on the left. The nature reserve is worth a quick detour. This damp habitat attracts insects, which in turn attract birds. You might even spot a great crested newt. Take the gate ahead into a field and head uphill, keeping the fence on your left. At the top of the field, go through another gate and continue uphill. Turn right onto the clear path running along the hillside.

2 Follow this path through the woods then along the edge of a pasture. You can see the ridged outline of the British Camp hill fort ahead. The path becomes a track and then a tarmac drive. Follow it until you reach a minor road at **Evendine**.

> ⓘ Keep an eye out for basking reptiles as you walk on the hills and commons. Common lizards, slow worms, grass snakes and adders are sometimes seen.

3 Turn left onto the road, then in about 180m, turn right just before Upper House, onto their drive. Pass the house and continue over two stiles into a field. Cross to the corner of the fence ahead, then keep the fence and hedge on your left. Where the hedge bends left, head to the far left-hand corner of the field. This corner can get muddy. Cross the stile and bridge. Continue straight to the next stile. British Camp is in view ahead. From here, the path is less clear. Head straight across the grass aiming a few metres to the left of the

47

Walking near Wynd's Point

solitary oak tree. From about halfway, you will be able to see the stile and waymarker. Cross the stile and take the path steeply uphill through young trees, past the toilet block and to the road at **Wynds Point**. There is a hotel with a public bar directly ahead and a refreshment kiosk round the corner to your right.

4 Turn left along the road. Where the pavement runs out, cross the road and take the path that runs steeply uphill. Beyond a row of benches, follow the path round to the left and over the small hill ahead. Continue until the path almost meets another rising from the left.

5 Switch to the other path around the side of **Black Hill** ahead. The area below this point glows with bluebells in spring. Follow this path, keeping Black Hill on your right, with views across Herefordshire on your left. After about 300m, fork left, then continue on this stone path past the bench dedicated to Dorothy Kate Shorland as it gradually drops down the side of **Pinnacle Hill** towards the road.

> ⓘ *Midsummer Hill and British Camp were both Iron Age hill forts and may each have housed populations of over 1500 people.*

WALK 8 – WYNDS POINT (BRITISH CAMP) FROM COLWALL

The ridged outline of British Camp Iron Age hill fort

6 At the car park entrance, heading in the same direction, cross the road (Jubilee Drive) and take the left fork down Chase Road. Take the first driveway on the left and head right to the five-barred gates. Cross the right-hand gate using the unusual metal stile. The path leads downhill. At a junction of paths, dogleg left then right to continue downhill. At the end of the hedges, pass through the gate and head directly down across the field, through a few trees to a clear path through the woods. Turn right along the path, then retrace your route down the steps to the left, through the gate below, along the edge of the field and back to **Colwall** station.

> ⓘ *The Shire Ditch that runs along the hills marks the historic boundary between the lands of the Bishop of Hereford and the Earl of Gloucester.*

> **+ To lengthen**
>
> At Wynds Point, cross to the British Camp car park and follow Walk 6 to visit British Camp hill fort, then return to Waypoint 4 to complete this route. The length of the combined walks is 8.5km (allow 4hr).

Looking back down the path to the car park

WALK 9
Holy Well from Gardiner's Quarry

Time: 2¼hr
Distance: 6km (3¾ miles)
Climb: 230m

Beautiful views, cool woodland and one of Malvern's most famous wells

Start/finish	Gardiner's Quarry
Locate	WR13 6DN ///stems.staples.offices
Cafes/pubs	Cafe just downhill from car park, hotel at Waypoint 4, pub and cafe at Wyche Cutting
Transport	Infrequent bus 675 from Malvern (Old Wyche Road stop) to join walk at Waypoint 5
Parking	Car park at Gardiner's Quarry
Toilets	At Wyche Cutting

This walk starts with a stiff climb onto the hills, where a bench is well positioned for you to enjoy the lovely views. The route then drops down through the wooded eastern slopes of the Malvern Hills to Holy Well and continues through woodland to the Wyche Cutting, where another stiff climb leads you back onto the ridge with more great views for the return journey. If you are staying at The Cottage in the Wood hotel, join the route at Waypoint 4.

Holy Well buildings

SHORT WALKS ON THE MALVERN HILLS

1 From the entrance to the car park with your back to the road, take the gravel path diagonally right uphill. Ignore the first path to the left. At the second junction, head right, now climbing less steeply. At the top of this path, climb a few stone steps and turn right. At a fork by a bench, turn left uphill, where you will find another bench partway up **Pinnacle Hill**.

> This is a great place to take a rest and admire the view to the left over the Severn Plain to the Cotswolds, ahead to British Camp hill fort and right over Herefordshire to Wales.

2 Head straight down the hill in front of the bench and before the path starts to rise again, switchback left then right onto a path heading gently downhill. Follow this gravel path as it switches back to the left. The hill is now rising on your left. At a junction with a wider gravel path, continue straight ahead, fairly flat. At a distinct fork, head right. The path

> ⓘ *The Malvern Hills are famous for their water. The rocks are not permeable, so the water travels through cracks and doesn't pick up any minerals.*

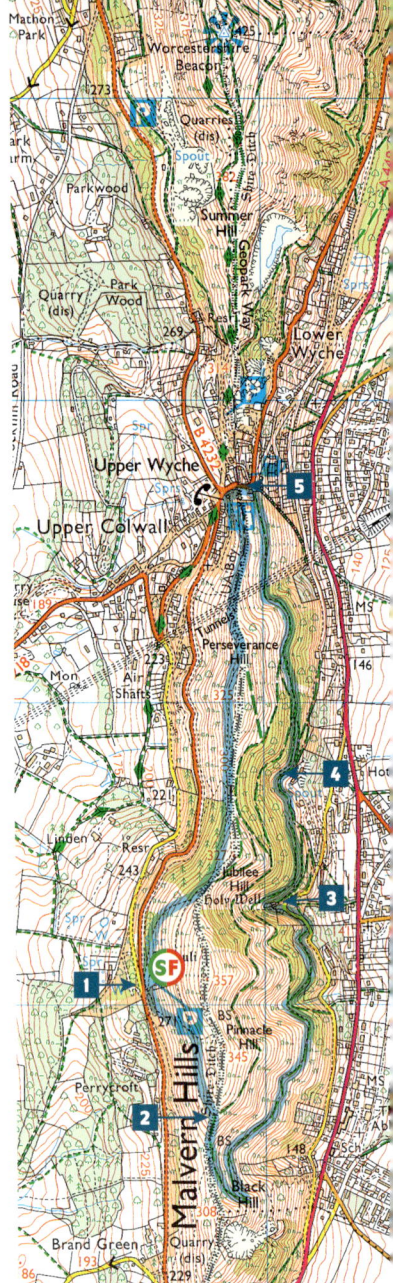

WALK 9 – HOLY WELL FROM GARDINER'S QUARRY

Holy Well

dips down and up again (ignore the path on the right that heads away downhill). Eventually, this path meets a quiet lane. Turn left to a cluster of buildings. **Holy Well** is housed in the building with a weathervane.

> The water that flows from the springs all around the Malvern Hills is famous for being so pure that it contains nothing else at all. Water was being bottled at Holy Well as early as 1622 and is again today.

3 As you leave the building containing the well, turn left following the sign for Holywell Cottage. Where paths cross by a bench and yew tree, fork left along the side of the hill. At the next junction, follow the wooden fence on your right. The Cottage in the Wood hotel is down on the right. To visit the hotel, continue to follow the wooden fence until you reach the gate.

A path along the hill

4 If you are not visiting the hotel, fork left at the next junction, away from the fence line. Continue in the same direction, around the hill, for about 1km to the road at **Upper Wyche**.

5 Turn left through the Wyche Cutting and left again up steps immediately before the bus stop. This path leads onto the hills, heading south.

Woodland path near Cottage in the Wood

WALK 9 – HOLY WELL FROM GARDINER'S QUARRY

A distant view of British Camp

You are now on **Perseverance Hill**, and Jubilee Hill is ahead. Our route takes you slightly to the right of the ridge. Alternatively, you can walk along the ridge. Both options meet on the far side of **Jubilee Hill**, where there is a stand of larches on the right. After the trees, take the right fork downhill, then just a few metres further along, take another right. This path heads steadily downhill back to Gardiner's Quarry.

+ To lengthen

Immediately after the Wyche Cutting, turn right instead of left to join the start of Walk 5 to the top of Worcestershire Beacon. The combined distance is 10km (4hr).

On the path between Hollybush and Whiteleaved Oak

WALK 10
The Southern Hills

Time: 3hr
Distance: 7.5km (4¾ miles)
Climb: 340m

Discover the quieter, less imposing southern hills, with fabulous views

Start/finish	Hollybush
Locate	HR8 1ET ///bloomers.upset.devours
Cafes/pubs	None on route
Transport	None nearby
Parking	Car park at Hollybush
Toilets	No public toilets on route

This walk has a different character to the others on the Malvern Hills. The southern hills are less busy, although still popular with those who prefer a more intimate landscape. With a good mixture of woodland and open vistas, the first part of the route takes you up Midsummer Hill, and the second part up the most southerly of the Malverns, Chase End Hill.

Walking north from Midsummer Hill

SHORT WALKS ON THE MALVERN HILLS

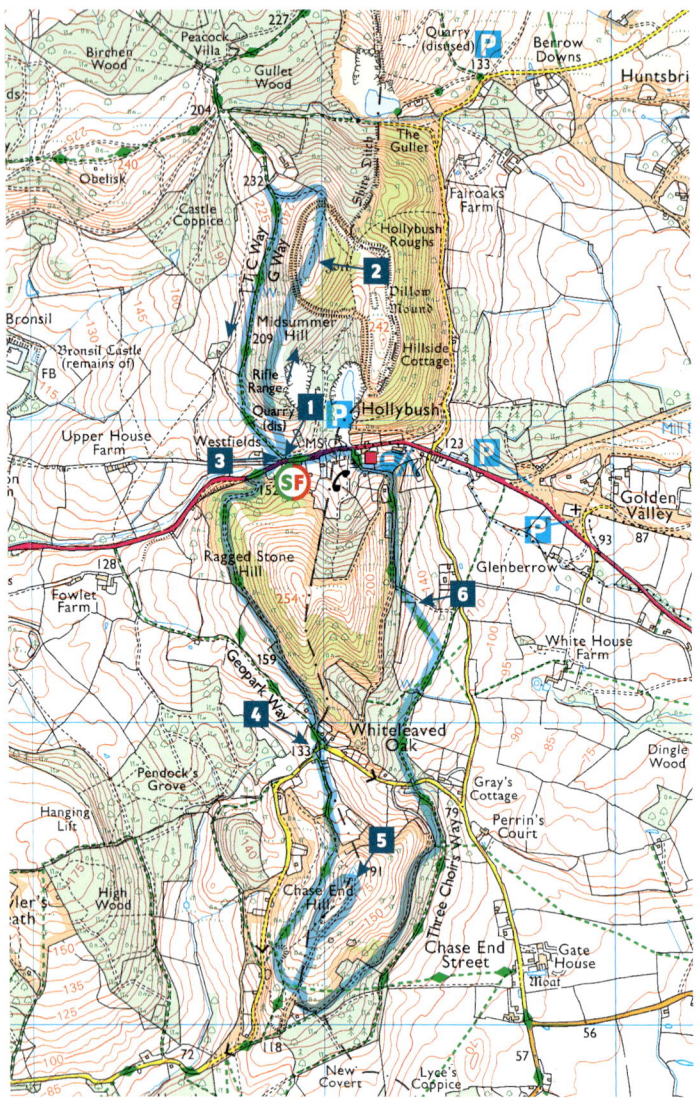

WALK 10 – THE SOUTHERN HILLS

1 From the car park, head through a gate up the steep grassy slope towards and then through a woodland. The path becomes gravelly before the tree line – if you are still on a grassy path when you reach the trees, move further left. The path eventually flattens off and opens up. Continue uphill to the summit of **Midsummer Hill**. Look left for a view of the obelisk (see Walk 11) and Eastnor Castle. From the top of the hill, the line of the Malvern Hills can be seen running north.

> Midsummer Hill is an Iron Age hill fort. It is highly unusual because it encloses two hills with a ravine between the two, housing a spring. There were 483 buildings here, which suggests a significant population.

2 From the summit continue north, towards the hills and through the ramparts. The gravel path heads downhill, bending to the left. At the bottom, turn left onto a stone track that becomes a tarmac lane and leads round the hill back down to the car park at **Hollybush**.

3 Turn right onto the A road. After about 120m, take the gate on the left. Immediately after the gate, fork right. At a junction of paths, bear right, keeping the hill on your left. After some distance, the path gently descends and then forks. Take the right fork downhill, past a garden on the right, through a gate and down to a track. Turn left to the road, passing some stocks on your right. They are fully functional, if you want to give them a go! This is the hamlet of **Whiteleaved Oak**.

Stocks at Whiteleaved Oak

4 Turn right along the road and take the first track on the left, past Cider Mill Cottage then up between hedges. Pass through a gate and continue ahead. Where the path starts to become steep and splits around some bushes, turn right round the hill, across a more open area. If you are feeling adventurous, continue straight up to the trig point instead of turning right. There are fine views to the south west from here. At the end of the open area, turn left at a junction of paths, keeping the hill on your left. At the fork, stay left, then turn left up the wide ride to the trig point on the top of **Chase End Hill**. This path splits and re-joins itself.

> ⓘ *The hills provide a home to 33 species of butterfly and 1117 species of moth. In early summer, dragonflies hunt all over the hills before returning to water to breed.*

5 From the summit, retrace your steps down the hill. As you near the woods, fork left and follow the path to the left, keeping the hill on your left. Ignore the gate on the right. Over some distance, the route passes through two wide gates. Just before the next, narrower gate (and before this path reaches a road), switchback

View over Herefordshire including Eastnor obelisk

right downhill. Pass through another small gate and turn left onto the wide path a few metres ahead. This path crosses the road on a bridge and eventually leads to a wide gate into a pasture. As you approach the second stand of trees in the pasture, turn diagonally left uphill past the dead tree and through the gate in the corner of the field. Note: this short section of path leads slightly to the right of the public footpath marked on the map and is not visible on the ground.

6 Pass another gate on your right, continue uphill for a short distance, then through the small gate ahead. Turn diagonally right to meet the track. Follow the track with the hill on your left for some distance until it reaches the road at Hollybush. Turn left to return to the car park.

> **— To shorten**
>
> This walk can easily be split into two separate loops. Allow 1hr for Midsummer Hill (2km) and 2hr for Chase End Hill (5.5km).

Eastnor obelisk

WALK 11
Eastnor obelisk

Start/finish	*The Woodshed, Eastnor*
Locate	*HR8 1RA ///chitchat.greet.abode*
Cafes/pubs	*Cafe at start*
Transport	*None nearby*
Parking	*Public car park at start*
Toilets	*At start*

Time: 1¾hr
Distance: 5km (3 miles)
Climb: 180m

An easy walk on good paths through a parkland landscape with a climb to Eastnor obelisk

A pretty walk through Eastnor Deer Park, this takes you between a couple of lakes that are home to wildlife such as birds and dragonflies and up a slope to the obelisk, with great views of Eastnor Castle on the return. The paths through the deer park are sometimes closed when the estate is hosting events – please check their website (https://eastnorcastle.com/eastnor-deer-park/) and follow signs on the ground during these periods.

The lake at Eastnor Deer Park

SHORT WALKS ON THE MALVERN HILLS

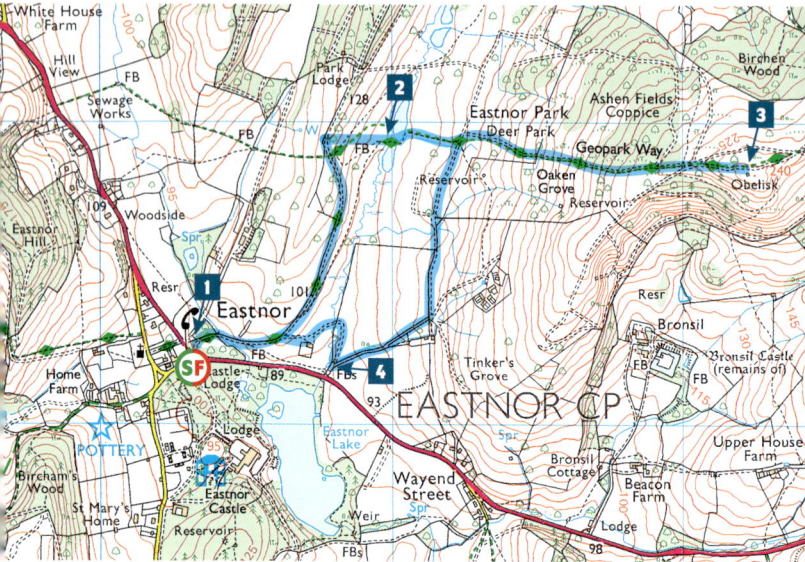

1 From The Woodshed, walk up the tarmac drive into the **deer park**. Remain on the tarmac drive as it curves up the slope. Opposite a kissing gate on the left, turn right across the concrete pad and head down the slope to the footbridge. The concrete pads were used as the base for Nissan huts to house American soldiers taking part in the D-Day landings in WWII.

2 Cross the bridge and continue between the lakes. Keep the second lake on your left for a few metres, then bear right to follow the hedge on your right gently uphill to the tarmac drive.

Dogleg left then right to take the track up the hill to the **obelisk**.

> The obelisk looks like it is solid but is actually hollow. The Napoleonic Wars (1803–1815) were raging when Eastnor Castle was being built, and this is a monument to the Earl's son who died in the conflict.

3 Return down the track to the tarmac drive you crossed earlier. Turn left onto the drive and follow it round the park until you reach gates to the road. There are great views of Eastnor Castle from this part of the route.

WALK 11 – EASTNOR OBELISK

Heading back down to the deer park from the obelisk

Building work started on Eastnor Castle in 1812. It was designed to impress and reflect the standing of the family, rather than act as a fortification. Ownership has remained in the same family for over 200 years.

4 Do not go through the gates to the road, but turn right back into the deer park and continue to follow the tarmac drive past the bowling clubhouse.

At the junction of drives, turn left to retrace your steps back to the cafe and the start.

– To shorten

Miss out the climb to the obelisk by turning right onto the tarmac drive mentioned in Waypoint 2, instead of crossing it, and continue the walk.

Eastnor Castle

Strolling through the meadow

WALK 12
St Wulstan's Nature Reserve

Time: 1hr
Distance: 2.5km (1½ miles)
Climb: 30m

A flat walk with meadows, woodland and great views of the hills

Start/finish	St Wulstan's Nature Reserve, Malvern Wells
Locate	WR14 4JA ///innovate.memory.protected
Cafes/pubs	None on route
Transport	None nearby
Parking	Car park at start
Toilets	No public toilets on route. Nearest at Wynd's Point

This easy, totally flat walk with plenty of benches also has plenty to delight the senses. The cool shade of the trees is enhanced by the sheer variety of species because of the unusual history of the site. In contrast, the open meadows are full of movement and colour in spring and summer, all with a stunning backdrop of the Malvern Hills.

Walking towards the Malvern Hills

SHORT WALKS ON THE MALVERN HILLS

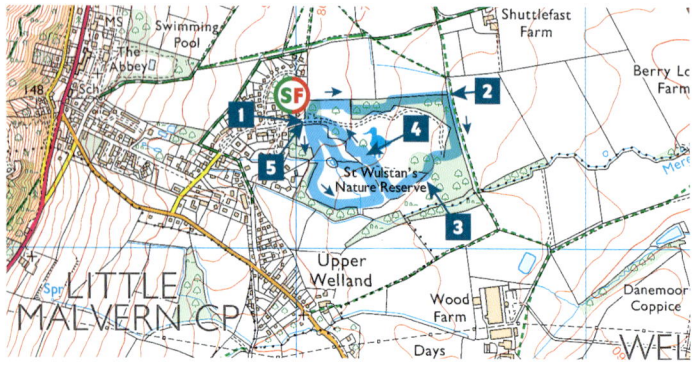

1 Take the small gate from the far corner of the car park into the woodland. After around 20m, turn right. Follow this path as it continues through the woods with open fields visible on the left to arrive at a junction of paths just before a small wooden bridge.

2 Without crossing the bridge, follow the path to the right, remaining in the woods with a field a few metres to your left. Some 200m further along, stay on the path as it bends to the right, away from the field. Pass a gate and reach a second gate on your right.

The distinctive Blue Atlas cedar

3 Follow the main path through this gate into a more open area, towards and then to the left of a distinctive Blue Atlas cedar, which is blue in colour as well as name and stands alone. Just before the path continues into a large open meadow, take the tarmac path to the right, back into the trees.

4 At a T-junction of paths, stay left on the main path. At the next junction, turn left again, keeping the meadow

The Malvern Hills rising beyond the nature reserve

in sight through the trees on your left. This path returns you to the car park.

5 At the car park, go through the gate into the large meadow. Take the right fork, cross a small footbridge and continue anticlockwise around the meadow to reach the car park once more. There are fabulous views of the hills from the second part of this loop.

— To shorten

This walk can easily be split into two loops. Allow 40min for the larger loop and 20min for the smaller one.

St Wulstan's Nature Reserve

It's hard to imagine it now, but during WWII, the farmland at St Wulstan's was turned into a field hospital for American soldiers injured in the D-Day landings. After the war, it was used as a training ground, a tuberculosis hospital and then a psychiatric hospital. When the hospital was demolished, many of the plants and trees from its grounds were incorporated into the nature reserve, which is why there is such a mix of native and exotic plants here. Many of the exotic plants enhance wildlife value, for example by providing early pollen for insects.

Heading up the gentle slope of Peachfield Common

WALK 13
Around Malvern Common

Start/finish	Peachfield Road, Malvern
Locate	WR14 4AL ///glove.games.soak
Cafes/pubs	Pub and cafe on Poolbrook Road
Transport	Train to Great Malvern station, around 1.5km from start
Parking	Car park opposite 58 Peachfield Road. If full, use other car parks or on-road parking on Peachfield Road
Toilets	No public toilets on route

Time: 1¾hr
Distance: 3.5km (2¼ miles)
Climb: 105m

An easy walk around flower-rich meadows with far-reaching views over the Severn Plain and the Cotswold Hills

A gentle walk on the eastern flank of the Malvern Hills around two commons, both marked on OS maps as Malvern Common. Peachfield Common, the higher of the two, is dominated by bracken and features a wide ride traversing the upper slope with far-reaching views. Lower down, Poolbrook Common is a meadow brimming with wildflowers, butterflies and the sound of skylarks in late spring and early summer.

View from the top part of Malvern Common

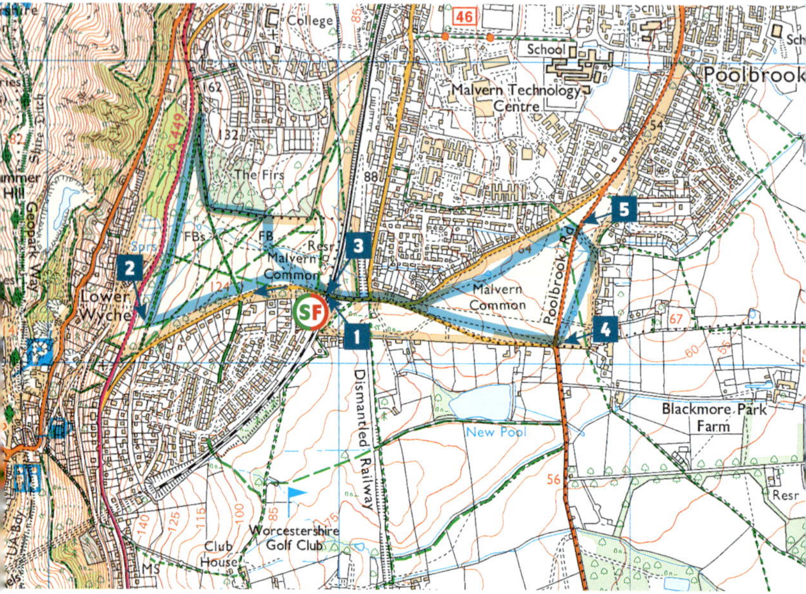

SHORT WALKS ON THE MALVERN HILLS

The wide grassy ride at the top of Malvern Common

WALK 13 – AROUND MALVERN COMMON

1 From the car park, take the path that rises up Peachfield Common towards the wooded slopes of the Malvern Hills. Continue uphill with the trees lining the road a few metres to your left, past a larger car park halfway up the common to a small one at the top.

2 Turn right onto the wide grassy ride that runs along the side of the hill. When the path becomes enclosed by trees, take the clear switchback to the right onto a lower track. Follow the garden wall on your left as it turns to the left and the view opens up again. Lower down, the wall is replaced by railings. At the junction of paths by a gap in the railings, take the second right that runs slightly downhill across the common. Cross a small stream, then head diagonally left back to the car park at the bottom of the slope.

3 For the second part of the walk, turn left onto the pavement, cross the railway bridge and continue downhill. The Victorian postbox ahead is Grade II listed because of its unusual fluted column. Pass the postbox, keeping Peachfield Road on your right. Walk down the grassy verge, cross three driveways and then a side road onto the main body of Poolbrook Common. Continue in the same direction until you reach **Poolbrook Road**.

4 Cross the road, then follow the path down and diagonally to the left. After a few metres, turn left and follow this

Victorian postbox between the two parts of the common

SHORT WALKS ON THE MALVERN HILLS

Orchid on Malvern Common

> ⓘ *Most of the Malvern Hills are a Site of Special Scientific Interest because of the wide diversity of rocks.*

5 Take a diagonal left towards a clump of trees about 250m away. This is a good place to see orchids in early summer. Cross a bridge then head diagonally right towards the same clump of trees. The path passes to the left of the trees and a small **pond** as it climbs gently back to the top of the common. Bear right in front of the houses and retrace your steps past the postbox, over the railway bridge and back to the car park.

path across the lower part of Poolbrook Common between the houses below and the road to the left. Continue across Hayes Bank Road. The second time the path intercepts Hayes Bank Road, turn left onto the road and cross back over Poolbrook Road.

> **− To shorten**
>
> This walk can easily be split into two separate loops. Allow 45min for the upper section and 1hr for the lower.

Malvern Common

Malvern Common is a nationally important species-rich grassland. Over winter, it looks like a grassy field, but in spring, it bursts into life with colourful wildflowers. In summer, the meadow buzzes with life and hosts clouds of Marbled White butterflies with their distinctive black-and-white markings. Towards autumn, the hay is cut and the cycle starts again. Listen for the distinctive 'space-invaders' song of skylarks, high in the sky. These delightful birds nest on the ground from April to August – please keep dogs on a lead and stick to the paths during this period to avoid disturbing the nesting birds.

WALK 14
Malvern Community Woodland

Time: 45min
Distance: 2.5km (1½ miles)
Climb: 25m

Start/finish	Malvern retail park off Townsend Way, Malvern
Locate	WR14 1PZ ///starting.twins.snowstorm
Cafes/pubs	Cafes at retail park
Transport	Train to Malvern Link station, about 1.5km from start. Bus from Malvern and Worcester
Parking	At retail park
Toilets	At retail park

Open views of the hills combine with the sights and sounds of maturing woodland on an easy circular walk

Leave the bustle of the town behind with this delightful amble by a stream, across some fields with great views of the hills and back along a broad path through a mixed woodland. Unusually for Malvern, this walk is almost completely flat. There are no benches on which to sit and rest, although there is an occasional felled tree in the woodland.

Horse grazing near the entrance to the woodland

Bluebells carpet the woodland in spring

WALK 14 – MALVERN COMMUNITY WOODLAND

One of the entrances to the woodland

1 From the car park, cross at the pedestrian crossing over Townsend Way. Follow the gravel path along the road for a few metres, then left into the woodland. After a short distance, the path bends to the right. Turn off the path to continue straight ahead through a gate into a field.

2 Follow the left edge of the field as it arcs to the right, following the line of a stream in the trees towards the far corner of the field. Before you reach the corner, look right to see the ridge of the Malvern Hills silhouetted against the sky.

The grand buildings glimpsed through the trees to your left as you enter the field are the Beauchamp Community – retirement homes built in 1864 and now run by an almshouse charity.

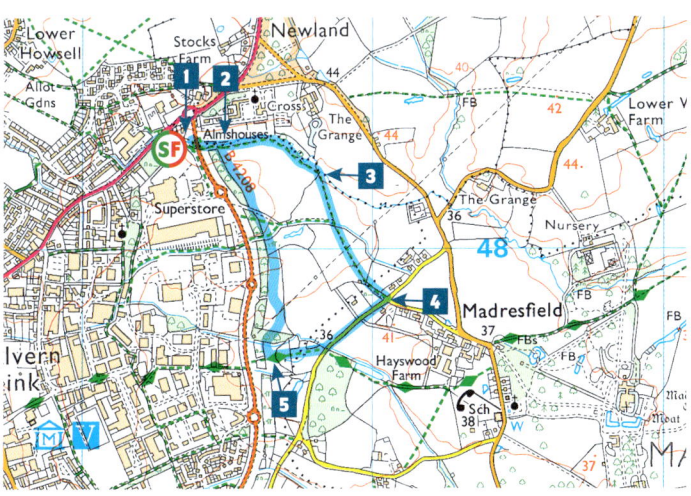

SHORT WALKS ON THE MALVERN HILLS

View of the hills

3 Cross the footbridge in the corner. There is a short waymarker just visible across this field when the crop and grass is short – look slightly to the right of the centre point between the two pylons. The footpath heads directly to this post, but most people walk around the edge, keeping the hedge on their right. At the waymarker, cross the land bridge over the drainage ditch and follow the clear path that runs diagonally left across the field, crossing underneath the power cables. Bear left to a gate and a minor road, North End Lane.

The path crosses a number of bridges

WALK 14 – MALVERN COMMUNITY WOODLAND

> ⓘ *The Malvern Hills were formed when ancient rocks were pushed upwards. This forced the land to fold in the west and drop in the east, creating the spectacular landscape we see today.*

Malvern Community Woodland

The narrow strip of Malvern Community Woodland is a haven for both wildlife and people. Most of the trees are young, although there are some big and gnarly ancient specimens of oak and willow, particularly along the streams and drainage ditches. Most of these older trees have been pollarded – cut about 2m above the ground to allow regrowth where cattle and deer can't reach the shoots. Keep an eye out for bluebells in spring, butterflies along the wide rides, small birds flitting from tree to tree and woodpeckers swooping between them.

4 Turn right onto North End Lane, a quiet road heading towards the hills. Immediately after crossing a small stream, turn right through a gate at the public footpath sign. Cross a couple of small paddocks into the community woodland.

5 Turn right onto the gravel path and cross a wooden bridge. At the second wooden bridge, cross it to remain on the correct route. After that, stay on the main path until you reach the end of the woodland. You will be able to see the pedestrian crossing on your right.

The path through the woodland

View from the trig point

WALK 15
Old Hills

Time: 1½hr
Distance: 3.5km (2¼ miles)
Climb: 25m

A gentle climb through a meadow, dropping into woodland where horses graze, with views to Worcester and the Malvern Hills

Start/finish	Upper Old Hills car park, Callow End
Locate	WR2 4TQ ///trumpet.lollipop.restore
Cafes/pubs	Pubs and hotel in Callow End
Transport	Infrequent bus 363 from Worcester (Pixham Ferry Lane stop)
Parking	Upper Old Hills car park (free)
Toilets	No public toilets on route

Old Hills is a popular destination for horse-riders and Sunday strollers. A gentle climb takes you to the ridge of the hill, where there are far-reaching views. There's a good chance of seeing horses as you drop down through the woods before circling through the village close to the pub and back to the car park. Some paths can become muddy.

Old Hills is a popular horse-riding area

SHORT WALKS ON THE MALVERN HILLS

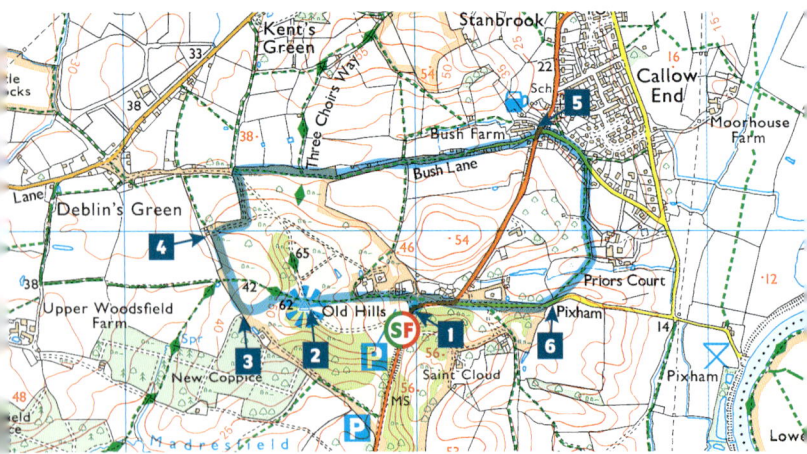

View of the Malvern Hills from Old Hills

WALK 15 – OLD HILLS

1 From the entrance to the car park, take the track slightly downhill towards the row of houses. Follow the track to the left, keeping the houses on your right. Ignore the turning to the right. At the end of the track, continue uphill past 110 Old Hills, 'The Loose Moose'. At first, keep the open grass to your left and scrub to your right, then head for the white trig point of **Old Hills** ahead. At the trig point, turn around for far-reaching views across the gentle hills of the Severn Plain.

2 Follow the path down a shallow valley away from the trig point. After a few metres, take the left fork. From here, there are views across to the Malvern Hills ahead. Follow this path down to the gate visible at the bottom of the slope.

3 Turn right along the wide green ride. There is a bench here, perfectly positioned to enjoy the view of the Malvern Hills. Keeping the Malverns to your left, continue along the ride, ignoring side-paths, until you reach a white house, 111 Old Hills.

4 Turn right onto their gravel drive and follow it to the left over a rise and down to a gate. Just before the gate, turn right in front of the hedge. Follow this path as it becomes a track (Bush Lane), enters the village of **Callow End** and meets the main road.

> ⓘ *The Berkley's Earthstar mushroom was thought to be extinct until it was recorded near some elm stumps at Old Hills in the late 1990s.*

5 At the road, dogleg left and then right down Upper Ferry Lane. After around 220m, take the narrow gravel path just before number 20 (Priorsfield) and enter the field at the end. Keeping the hedge to your left, pass through two more gates. Head diagonally right to cross the drainage ditch and continue to the far right-hand corner of the field.

6 Turn right onto the lane (Pixham Ferry Lane) back to the main road. Cross and turn left onto the footpath, past the postbox, to return to the car park.

+ To lengthen

At Waypoint 6 turn left along Pixham Ferry Lane. This will take you down to a picnic spot by the River Severn, where a ferry used to cross. Return along Pixham Ferry Lane to re-join the route. This adds 1km.

View over fields to the north of Old Hills

Old Hills common land

In the past, Old Hills was used by local people to graze livestock. The area is not fenced, so as the road got busier, keeping sheep here became less viable. As grazing declined, trees and scrub started to grow, impacting on some of the grassland species. These days, the Malvern Hills Trust uses a combination of mowing and grazing by highland cattle to maintain the grassland. Some locals still graze tethered horses here, and it is a popular horse-riding area.

USEFUL INFORMATION

Tourism bodies

Visit the Malverns www.visitthemalverns.org/attraction/malvern-hills/
Malvern Hills Trust www.malvernhills.org.uk/visiting/

Tourist information

Malvern tourist information centre, Church Street, Malvern,
(just below Great Malvern Priory), tel 01684 892289

Geopark Way Visitor Centre, Walwyn Road, Upper Colwall,
tel 01684 252414, www.geocentre.co.uk/.
For information, cafe and hire of an all-terrain tramper wheelchair.

Travel

www.traveline.info/

Accommodation

www.booking.com
www.trivago.co.uk
www.airbnb.co.uk

Clockwise from top: View of North Hill from the path down (Walk 5); The buzzards sculpture in Rose Bank Gardens (Walks 1 and 2); Hangman's Hill and Midsummer Hill from British Camp (Walk 6); Looking back down the track leading to the obelisk (Walk 11)

NOTES

© Julia Goodfellow-Smith 2023
First edition 2023
ISBN: 978 1 78631 139 9

Printed in Singapore by KHL Printing using responsibly sourced paper.
A catalogue record for this book is available from the British Library.

© Crown copyright 2023 OS PU100012932
All photographs are by the author unless otherwise stated.

CICERONE

Cicerone Press, Juniper House, Murley Moss, Oxenholme Road,
Kendal, Cumbria, LA9 7RL

www.cicerone.co.uk

Updates to this Guide

While every effort is made to ensure the accuracy of guidebooks as they go to print, changes can occur during the lifetime of an edition. Any updates that we know of for this guide will be on the Cicerone website (www.cicerone.co.uk/1139/updates), so please check before planning your trip. We also advise that you check information about transport, accommodation and shops locally. We are always grateful for updates, sent by email to updates@cicerone.co.uk or by post to Cicerone, Juniper House, Murley Moss, Oxenholme Road, Kendal, LA9 7RL.

Register your book: To sign up to receive free updates, special offers and GPX files where available, register your book at www.cicerone.co.uk.